THE
GOOSE
FROM SCARSDALE

By
Clive Howard

LYLE STUART, INC.
SECAUCUS, NEW JERSEY

To Isabel,
And to all the animals in our household, past and
present.
To the horses, King and Duke and Hurricane.
And the dogs, Doc and Greta and Brandy.
And the cats, Lightning and Andrew.
Sad to say, we never owned a goose.

PREFACE

So that you may enjoy this little book more fully, let me first explain about George Reichart.

George is the vice-president in charge of advertising for the General Cigar Company, New York, which you will more easily identify through its advertising—its television commercials particularly—for Tiparillos, White Owls, Tijuana Smalls, and some other famous cigar brands, very far-out stuff for an industry which is generally thought to be stodgy and old fashioned. At one time or another, this advertising has won just about every award there is for excellence, which makes George one of the more celebrated company advertising directors.

There is nothing flagrantly Madison Avenue about George Reichart, however. In all his business discussions, and in his voluminous memoranda, he manages to convey his thoughts clearly without ever leaning on the industry's crutch vocabulary, on words and phrases like demographics or psychographics or gross rating points.

George is rather slight of build; he talks in even, unhurried tones and at the age of 62 still has most of his hair, which is auburn, with some gray, and wavy. He wears glasses with a light-gray transparent frame. He dresses conservatively, although if the occasion demands, he will cut loose with a brightly colored shirt and splashy necktie.

Naturally, he is almost never seen without a cigar, which he handles with the grace of a symphony conductor fingering his baton.

I know George in that special and complete way one man gets to know another when they travel together constantly on business, sharing taxis and rented cars, waiting around airports, locked together in side-by-side seats through endless flying hours, eating breakfast, dinner, and lunch together. On and off for sixteen months, George and I traveled to thirty-four cities introducing his company's newest product, Tijuana Smalls.

George's company had retained me to publicize Tijuana Smalls; George was the company spokesman. My job was to stage the luncheon and cocktail parties and turn out the television, newspaper, and radio people. George's job was to convince them.

I had been told that George was a funny and effective speaker and much in demand for cigar industry functions. I was not impressed. I have seen too many executives, self-assured and articulate in their own environment, completely choke up when they face an editorial audience. They talk as if their underwear is too tight.

Not George, though. He gets to his feet looking meek and uncertain, as if he wonders what he is doing here, and who are all these other people and what are they doing here. He starts out in a downcast tone, like the actor Jimmy Stewart addressing a joint session of Congress, as he pleads the problems of the cigar business. Particularly, the problems with Hollywood.

"The people out there, anytime they are casting a gangster, they just take any old actor and they stick a cigar in his face, and he is an instant Al Capone." Sorrowfully, George informs his audience that the cigar industry never had enough advertising money to combat that kind of image.

Then, his voice brightening, George tells about the time his company got very modern and researched its youth market. His voice hits bottom again as he informs the audience that it turned out the industry's youth market started at age forty-seven.

Gradually, slyly—scattering wry witticisms all over the luncheon premises—George gets to Tijuana Smalls and how it will change all this. (It did, too.) Partly because George looks so meek and vulnerable, and because he is a crafty wit, everybody gets the message, in between gales of laughter. George Reichart is to the press luncheon circuit what George Gobel was to television.

In staging the luncheons, I learned early in the

tour to keep one eye on the clock and the other on George's upper lip. George is a martini drinker. Near the bottom of his second martini, his upper lip freezes as though shot with novocaine, and his nose twitches. That means it is time to close the bar.

In Miami, at the Playboy Club, things got away from me, and George made it almost to the end of his third martini before I cut off the drinks. He then thanked everyone for coming to the lunch. That was standard. "I know each of you had a telegram of invitation from our president, Mr. Edgar Cullman. He has asked me to apologize for his absence. He is in New York, detained by business." That was standard, too. Edgar Cullman is a very busy man.

"Frankly," George told all the people from the press, "we are damn lucky he isn't here."

There was a momentary, collective gasp—followed by an explosion of laughter. No one there had ever heard a company representative put down his president out loud and on the record. But the loudest laughter of all was the echoing guffaw in the New York City headquarters of the General Cigar Company, from the office of the president.

The only certainty about traveling with George is its uncertainty. If, for example, you arrive at an airport terminal with only minutes to spare and your gate is farthest from the entrance, George holds to the pace of a pallbearer with a fractured tibia. He feels constrained to examine the inventory of the airport tobacco stand and, if possible, to develop a conversation with whomever is in charge on the state of the cigar business, by brand and by size and by shape and by price.

George loses or misplaces everything that isn't buttoned, belted, or laced to his body: his suitcase, his briefcase, his raincoat, his plane ticket. Somehow, though, he gets where he is going. Eventually.

His attitude toward business meetings in New York is equally casual. If, for example, it is now quarter to three in the afternoon and a meeting was scheduled to begin back at the office fifteen minutes ago, but the luncheon conversation has taken a fascinating direction, George will relight his cigar, order another cup of coffee and resume the conversation.

I would not say that George is by nature rebellious, or deliberately a nonconformist. I think he is sort of indifferent. Possibly the reason he gets away with it is that he is very good at his job.

George is also artistically talented, as is his wife, Jane. Both are exhibiting members of the local art association in Scarsdale, New York, where they live. Jane's watercolors win blue ribbons and sell fairly well. George's hardly ever win blue ribbons but sell like hot dogs at a ball game.

Jane's paintings, like those of most members of the Scarsdale Art Association, are landscapes. George paints the Old West, horses, and Indians. His theory is that this is the first long interval in history when man and his horse have been separated; therefore man is subconsciously lonesome for his horse.

Besides, the Old West is familiar territory to George. He was born in 1910, two days after Christmas, in a homesteader's shack on the Rosebud Indian reservation in South Dakota.

There are some remarkable things about George's horses. Jane says they look like stuffed horses because they have big, round behinds and fat bellies. Indeed, an Indian fleeing the white man on one of George's horses couldn't make it to the next corner, even with a head start.

More remarkably, George's horses and Indians don't always add up right. One of his earliest paintings showed three horses, but Jane counted fourteen legs. Another showed two horses but only five legs. A recent work shows some Indians on horses at dusk, beginning the long descent into a shadowed canyon. Depending on how you look at it, there are four Indians on three horses or four Indians on five horses. George's argument is that he is striving for effect, so who cares if there are not enough legs to go around, or too many legs, or not enough Indians, or too many Indians?

It must be that whatever effect George is striving for in his paintings, he achieves; you can study any one of them at length without noting an inconsistency.

Occasionally, George's sideline art career affords the opportunity to display his merchandising inventiveness. As the Scarsdale Art Association's annual outdoor show went into its last day this past fall, there were many paintings left unsold, including an even dozen of the Reicharts'. Attendance had been thin, and there were many more lookers than buyers. Around noon, George disappeared; he was at home in the downstairs studio lettering a big sign which he put out in front of the Reichart booth.

"Buy a George or Jane Reichart," the sign announced. "You may win fifty thousand dollars." Taped to each painting was a ticket for the New York State Lottery. By closing time, all the Reichart paintings were sold. One man paid two hundred dollars for one of Jane's paintings, a big bowl of fruit. "Hate fruit," he explained, "but that number has three sevens in it."

"Supposing," Jane told George, "one of those numbers actually does win fifty thousand dollars. I should think you'd want to cut your throat."

"Maybe," George conceded, "and maybe not. Just think of it. One of us could be the first member in the history of the Scarsdale Art Association with a painting worth fifty thousand dollars."

Early in my travels with George, I learned that he is a raconteur of extraordinary facility. There is scarcely any comment or incident that does not serve to remind him of some experience or other from his boyhood in South Dakota, or from his years as a cigar salesman, or his adventures as an advertising man, or his vacations with Jane in places like Algiers, or

Morocco, or Tunisia, or even the Sahara Desert, where he went one June because he thought it would be less crowded then.

Like any dedicated raconteur, George tells a story as much for his own pleasure as his listener's, so he is likely to repeat a story, not once, but several times. If you interrupt George to say that you've heard this one, he reacts like a man with a hearing aid whose battery has gone dead. He pauses only slightly, glances at you uncomprehendingly and proceeds with the story.

I thought I had heard all of George's experiences, but one day at lunch in New York long after our tour was ended, George began telling me about the little creature kingdom in his backyard in Scarsdale, about the birds and the squirrels and the skunks. And about the Goose.

I listened because the story is funny the way George tells it, but it is also something more than funny. It seems to me it is a wry commentary on what happens to people when they go to live in the suburbs, and a saddening chronology of the encroachment of the thing we call civilization upon the furred and feathered creatures of the forests; the endless forests which became scattered patches of woods, which became tidy lawns and sold millions of power mowers.

I hope you enjoy George's story about the Goose from Scarsdale for whatever its meaning. I hope it causes you to grin and chuckle and even laugh. And

14

perhaps, here and there, you will shake your head in sadness, as I did.

Most of all, when you come to the end of this, I hope you feel as I did when George came to its end.

I hope you feel warm all over.

Here then, as simply as George told it to me, is the story of the Goose from Scarsdale. The events recounted took place over a long period of time, a decade or so, but I have condensed them to avoid boresome repetition.

All the people in this book are real, and their names are their real names.

The illustrations, of course, are by George and Jane Reichart.

CHAPTER ONE

In the fall of 1957, the Reichart family, George and Jane and their little daughter, Jan, and the family pet—a basset hound named Ichabod—moved into their new home in a quiet neighborhood in Scarsdale, New York.

The house was a newly built split-level standing among homes of mixed design and vintage on Westminster Road, a short distance from Jan's new school, a few blocks from the stores on Central Avenue, and a five minute drive down the hill to the railroad station.

What the Reicharts liked most about their new home was the backyard, which sloped uphill, ending at the base of a heavily wooded hill. When they looked out through the picture window in the living room, which was at the back of the house, they could see only their own stretch of lawn and the woods. There were no other houses in sight or neighbors or even fences. It was like living in a forest.

But it wasn't anything like the house they had just

come from on Wood Drive in the hilly part of Oakland, California. In Oakland when you entered the house you stepped into an enormous living room with a picture window that ran the length of the house. Through the picture window to the right was the Golden Gate Bridge and at the far left, if the day was clear, you could see all the way down to Palo Alto. All of San Francisco was framed in the picture window and downtown Oakland and Lake Merritt and the bay. When the fog moved in low over the Bay Area, you could look down through the picture window onto the top of the fog cloud; then it was like living on a magic carpet moored onto nothingness. At night, as George describes it, "You'd look down and see all those lights twinkling. About fourteen million dollars worth of electricity going on down there every night, just for us."

None of the Reicharts wanted to leave California, or the house in Oakland, certainly not to go live anywhere near New York City. But there had been no way George could turn down his company's offer of the job as its advertising manager. He didn't know anything about advertising, he argued, all he knew was how to sell cigars. His boss, Philip Bondy, then the company's national sales manager, explained that what they needed was someone who understood the cigar business. Advertising was something George could learn as he went along; the advertising agency, a big one, would teach him that.

So the Reicharts had moved east to Scarsdale. Jan

began classes at Edgemont High School, Jane began studying watercolor painting, and George began commuting to New York to learn how to be an advertising man.

George got the full treatment. The advertising agency gave him an orientation course, and he wound up with a Brooks Brothers suit, some striped ties, and button-down shirts. He went to a lot of cocktail parties and lunches and began to get the feel of the executive approach to big business. He learned early in the orientation that in New York, in the advertising business, it can grow dark right in the middle of lunch.

Weekends, George worked at building a stone terrace and retaining wall that meandered across the rear of the yard and circled almost completely around the base of a big oak tree. He and Jane often sat out there, contentedly admiring the changing fall colors. They had no way of knowing then that their little backyard one day would be turned into the battleground for a very strange kind of neighborhood war.

Just before Christmas, as a way to introduce themselves to their new neighbors, they invited all the people living around them to a cocktail party. About forty people came, and almost everyone got loosened up on George's special get-acquainted punch, which is mostly brandy mixed with brandy, but there was something strange about the party. All evening, George and Jane found themselves introducing the neighbors to each other.

The Reicharts made some new acquaintances, but they were sad about the people who went to the same churches, who shopped in the same stores and even commuted to New York from the same railroad platform, but had to be introduced to each other by some new people who didn't know anybody either.

22

CHAPTER TWO

It started with the pheasants.

One morning not long after moving into the house in Scarsdale, George happened to look out the kitchen window and was amazed. There were some pheasants out back, pecking around like chickens in a farmyard.

This was something he had never seen in California. Here he was living only twenty-five miles from the middle of New York in practically a wilderness.

He counted four pheasants and called upstairs to Jane, "Boy, wait until you see this!"

In the stream down below the house, which was swampy and filled with cattails, he had seen some wild ducks while walking Ichabod. But a bunch of pheasants right outside the kitchen door—that was something else.

As soon as he arrived at the office that morning, he told Phil Bondy, "You know what we've got in our backyard? We've got pheasants running around. I saw four of them this morning. Imagine that, four pheasants!"

Phil, who lived twice as far from New York as George did and raised chickens and bred horses and dogs, was not at all impressed. All he said was, "Pheasants? What's so special about that?"

The next weekend George bought a bunch of cracked corn and birdseed and chicken feed and everything else he thought the pheasants might like. Naturally, when he went out to feed the pheasants in the morning, they ran into the woods. George tried putting the food out at night where the pheasants would find it in the morning.

They did, and every morning while George was eating breakfast, the pheasants were pecking away out in the backyard like a bunch of chickens. After a few days, a couple of other pheasants showed up and then some more and one morning about a month after he first saw them, there were fourteen pheasants feeding in the backyard.

George couldn't get over that. He hurried to the office and told Phil, "Boy, now you really won't believe what's going on at our house. We had fourteen pheasants out in our backyard this morning."

Phil was frowning at a stack of sales reports. "What are you getting to be?" he scowled. "Some kind of a professional bird watcher?"

George was crestfallen about Phil's attitude, but he figured that if you have a whole flock of pheasants running around in your backyard, and you don't notice them, you're some kind of a nut. He kept on putting out the food because it was so fascinating

24

to watch the pheasants in the morning, the cock pheasants particularly, with their gorgeous plumage.

There were some other birds around the yard. Deciding they ought to be fed, too, George built a bird feeding station. Jane bought a book which told how to attract birds and showed how to tell one species from another.

One day at the office, when George was in a meeting, Jane called up and told him, all out of breath, "George, you won't believe it, but do you know what we've got out on the bird feeding tray? George, we've got a titmouse."

George had never seen a titmouse—that was something else they didn't have in California—so he sneaked out of the office a little early and got home as fast as he could. First he cautioned Jane not to call him anymore at the office about birds, lest she tarnish his new image as an advertising man. "The secretaries down there," he told Jane, "don't know a titmouse is a bird. They were giggling all afternoon."

Soon, attracted by the pheasant's food, there were a few more titmice in and out of the backyard, and a few chickadees, and some other kinds of birds.

In November it turned cold and by December there was snow and ice; some mornings the temperature was down to eight degrees. Sitting inside the warm house at breakfast, looking out at the pheasants and birds moving around on top of the snow and ice, he would say to Jane, "God, how can they stand this weather. They'll freeze to death." He couldn't understand why they didn't go south. As far as he knew, all birds went south for the winter.

George put out a little extra food in case there were some more birds around not smart enough to take off for Florida. That brought a couple of squirrels into the backyard.

George experimented around with different kinds of food and discovered that squirrels—these squirrels at least—liked sunflower seeds.

Every night all that winter George put out the food for the pheasants and birds and tossed sunflower seed out for the squirrels. It was so cold at times, and there was so much snow, that he had to get all bundled up in heavy clothing and boots. Some nights, when he arrived home late from being wined and dined by someone from the advertising agency or a magazine or television or radio salesman, his booted footsteps made funny looking circles in the snow, and the food was scattered all over the place.

But always the next morning George would sit there in the nice warm breakfast room with a cup of hot coffee watching the birds and the pheasants and the squirrels feeding outside and looking like they were freezing to death.

It gave George a good feeling to think that, well, he was spending a few dollars to put out the food and birdseed and, well, so what's a few dollars if it helps some little animals get through the winter?

CHAPTER THREE

The following spring more and more birds were populating the Reicharts' backyard. There were more pheasants now than ever, and cardinals and blue jays and juncos and fox sparrows and nuthatches and some more. Jane joined the local chapter of the National Audubon Society and began keeping a record of all the different varieties and the dates they first turned up.

George figured there must have been a lot of word-of-mouth publicity going on in the bird world about the good thing that was going on over at the Reicharts'.

Perhaps so, because one morning around dawn, the Reichart household was awakened by a kind of machine-gun tattoo beating against the side of the house. There was a woodpecker up near the roof on one side of the house drilling away at a shingle. Jane identified him as a downy woodpecker. George was sure the woodpecker would soon go away. "Aw, what's a shingle," he told Jane, "if that's his thing, let him have the shingle."

Every morning, always at dawn, the drilling started up again. One morning, hoping the woodpecker would go away, George threw a rock up toward the roof. He missed the woodpecker and the rock crashed through a bedroom window. Finally, four or five shingles fell to the ground.

"Aw, what's four or five shingles anyhow?" he asked Jane.

"It isn't the shingles," Jane said. "It's the neighbors. They don't like being awakened every morning by a gang of woodpeckers."

Apparently woodpeckers attract woodpeckers. The quiet Scarsdale neighborhood began to pound like a city street being dug up by a repair crew.

George's friend from next door, Dr. Hans Havemann, was not only losing sleep but dozens of shingles. He bought a realistic-looking porcelain cat and perched it on a little ledge up near the roof of his house. Hans got rid of the woodpeckers, but they all went over to George's house. He thought about getting a porcelain cat, too, but that might scare away the birds landing in his backyard. Then somebody in the neighborhood told Jane that woodpeckers like worms and maybe the Reicharts' shingles were kind of buggy.

George called up the local building supply company and asked someone there if it was possible the woodpeckers came around because his shingles were buggy. "The problem is," George said, "they come around here at daybreak, and my wife gets mad, and the neighbors get mad, and it isn't creating what you might call much harmony in the neighborhood."

The building supply man explained that the woodpeckers were banging away at George's shingles because there were not enough dead trees around anymore. "Tell you what, though," he said, "somewhere I heard that woodpeckers like meat scraps and suet. Maybe if you feed it to them, they'll stay away from the shingles."

That struck George as a pretty good idea, except logistically it didn't sound practical. He couldn't quite see himself perched up on a stepladder at daybreak every morning, carrying a breakfast tray for the woodpeckers.

Finally, he bought some little mesh bags, stuffed them with a mixture of meat scraps, bones, and suet, and hung them out back in the trees. For awhile, the woodpeckers concentrated on the food in the mesh bags, but in time they were alternating between this and the shingles.

"I suppose," George told Jane, "it's something hereditary. They've just got to be knocking holes in something."

What bothered George far more than the woodpeckers was the nagging fear of the coming winter. He couldn't bear to think of all the birds—so many more now than the year before—living outdoors, freezing to death. He bought a book on how to make bird boxes, which said that if you make a box this big and this wide and this high, and you hang it exactly this many feet above the ground, the birds will use it but the squirrels will not.

George built the box, stained it, and very carefully hung it at exactly the right height. He hurried into the house and took his accustomed place at the breakfast table to make certain the birdhouse was in the line of his vision.

There was a big fat squirrel sitting on top of the bird box like he owned it. Which he did, in a way, because by spring there were four baby squirrels poking their tiny heads out of the bird box.

George didn't mind about the squirrels taking over the bird box. He assumed they were just part of the whole scheme of things.

CHAPTER FOUR

Time moved swiftly for the Reichart family.

Jan was graduated from Edgemont High School and went off to Antioch College and came home for Christmas vacation with her hair long and stringy and wearing a baggy old racoon coat she found in a thrift shop. Ichabod, the little basset hound, didn't recognize her, or maybe wasn't even sure what it was he was looking at; he barked at her, or it, or whatever it was.

Jane's watercolors had improved so markedly that they were winning quite a few blue ribbons.

George was doing well at his job; there was talk of making him a vice-president.

The Reicharts' backyard, in the meantime, had grown into a noisy wonderland of tiny creatures. There were some wild rabbits running about and some chipmunks and the squirrels, of course, but there were many more than the little family that nested in the bird box.

Jane's notebook was filled with page after page of the names of flying creatures; some were transient, others flew in and stayed. There were exotically beautiful species like the red-breasted nuthatch, the yellow-billed cuckoo, the black-throated blue warbler, the purple grackle, the parula warbler, the gray-cheeked thrush, the ruby-crowned kinglet, and even a pileated woodpecker. There were cardinals and blue jays and chickadees and sparrows.

There were, in all, fifty-five species on Jane's list of birds that had flown in to feed on the terrace out back. And twenty-eight that frequented the feeding trays up off the ground.

Looking out at all the feathery colors and their infinite gradations, and listening to all the chirping and whistling and pecking, George could not believe this really existed only twenty-five miles from New York. It was more like something right out of *Alice in Wonderland.*

Except for the woodpeckers, there were no problems with the neighbors, either. George and Jane's Christmas get-together had become an annual neighborhood tradition. The first couple of years the party was at the Reicharts' house. Then the high school principal, Ossie Laubenstein, who lived down the street, said he'd like to have the party at his house the next year. Then Bob Alexander and his wife, from a couple of doors away, held the party. Fred Kimball had the party the year he built the new game room down in the basement.

Everytime somebody was promoted, or when someone moved out, or moved in, there was a party. Now,
almost everybody in the neighborhood knew everybody else.

CHAPTER FIVE

There were other changes taking place, however. They occurred singly and were so spaced apart in time as to pass without notice. Then, as if it had all happened overnight, they fused together so that a former resident of Westminster Road, revisiting the neighborhood after a five year absence, might have had trouble finding the place.

The swampy stream down below the Reichart house where George used to walk Ichabod was all filled in and covered up by a big new supermarket. The Korvette discount chain built a huge store there, too. Up on top of the hill overlooking the Reicharts' backyard, the estate which had belonged to Walter Winchell was subdivided and a bunch of new homes were being built. The woods up there were all gone.

The pheasants disappeared from the Reicharts' backyard. Then, one by one, some of the more exotic and timid of the bird species disappeared. The flickers were gone and the red-winged blackbirds and the grackles and the warblers.

One morning a pigeon flew into the backyard and landed on the terrace. The next morning there were two pigeons out back, and within a week there were a dozen or more.

George wasn't exactly carried away by the idea of the pigeons using his place as a hangout, but as long as they had feathers and landed in his backyard, he felt they were entitled to some food.

The neighbors did care, though. One of the wives said to Jane, "You know, your husband is feeding pigeons. We don't think you should be attracting pigeons."

"Why not?" Jane asked.

"Well," the woman said, "because they're *pigeons*."

Jane told George and he got mad. "What do the neighbors care?" he wanted to know. "It's our backyard and it's none of their business. I don't complain about what they do in their backyards, do I? Besides, I'm not running a segregated bird-feeding joint around here."

George kept on feeding the pigeons and, of course, some more came. George and Jane figured the pigeons came up from the railroad station; there were a lot of them hanging around there. Standing on the station platform waiting for his train, which was hardly ever on time anymore, George was sure he could pick out the pigeons which dropped by his backyard.

40

CHAPTER SIX

Around November of the year the pigeons appeared for the first time, the new neighbor next door, Ed James, began shooting up the squirrels' nests in the big tree behind his house.

George liked Ed James, mostly because he was an interesting conversationalist. He was born in Portugal and grew up there, but every few years the big oil company for which he worked sent him to some other country. Ed and his family moved into the house where Hans Havemann had lived, after Hans moved back to Europe.

When George saw Ed shooting up the squirrels' nests he hurried over and said, "Look, Ed, why do you want to be shooting up the squirrels' nests, this time of year especially? You know if you keep that up they're going to end up in your attic because they don't have any place to spend the winter."

That made sense to Ed James, so he stopped. But the next Saturday morning George saw a big wire cage in Ed's backyard, and some traps which Ed was baiting with shelled peanuts. George realized the connection immediately; squirrels, he knew, like peanuts the way most children like pizza.

"Sure," Ed admitted. "I'm catching squirrels. We've got too many of them around here. I take them out into the woods, far enough so they won't find their way back here, and dump them off. We've got way too many of them around here."

George had to admit that if you put up a box and raise squirrels and feed them you are likely to end up with a few more squirrels than normal. But he hurried home and told Jane, "Look, Ed James is trying to trap our squirrels. We'd better feed them a lot so they won't run over into his backyard and get caught."

Jane doubted if this would work. "You can't stay home from work everyday to feed the squirrels, and I can't be home every minute, either." Even so, George and Jane put out food for the squirrels as often as they could.

It didn't help, though. One by one the squirrels were disappearing into Ed's cage. Jane felt terrible about it. They were the baby squirrels that were born in the little birdhouse. She had seen them the very first time they poked their noses out, and she had been feeding them every day and watching them grow. Now, they were being carried off into the woods, which were strange to them and probably terrifying.

By the end of winter, there was nobody at home anymore in the bird box that stood just outside the Reicharts' kitchen window.

CHAPTER SEVEN

George was sad about the squirrels, too. As it turned out, however, the skunks provided an endlessly fascinating summertime diversion.

George and Jane passed most of the summer nights sitting out on the big redwood deck they had built onto the back of the house. George had a television set there so he could watch the Mets baseball games. His company had bought some commercial time on the Mets telecasts to advertise White Owls and Tiparillos, and it was part of his job to make sure the commercials actually got on the air. The way the Mets played in those days, this wasn't exactly what you'd call a fringe benefit.

George saw the first skunk one night, moving around the terrace where all the bird feed was and whispered to Jane to look out back. She did, and lost all interest in the game. The skunk sampled some of the food, but apparently found it unappetizing and disappeared into the woods.

George remembered that he once knew a kid back

in South Dakota who had a pet racoon that was crazy about chocolate bars. The next evening he placed some chunks of chocolate out on the terrace. Later, he watched as the skunk came out of the woods, sniffed around the terrace, pawed at a piece of chocolate, ate it and then gobbled up all the rest. Every night after work George stopped at the newsstand in Grand Central Station to buy a couple of chocolate bars.

After awhile he decided it might be a good idea to vary the skunk's diet. He looked around the house and found a couple of packages of Fritos and put some out on the terrace. The skunk liked the Fritos even more than the chocolate. You could hear him chomping on them all the way up to the deck.

One night George dribbled a trail of Fritos from the terrace, through the backyard, and up a couple of steps onto the deck. A few hours later, the skunk came out from the woods, followed by another skunk.

The pair ate their way down the backyard right up onto the deck where George and Jane were sitting. While Jane froze and George looked on in wonderment—and the Mets played on—the skunks gobbled up all the Fritos. They hung around quite awhile before leaving, so George concluded that skunks liked the light and some noise around them. It was the most fun George ever had watching the Mets.

Of course, word got around the neighborhood that George was entertaining some skunks every night. Some woman told Jane that her husband shouldn't be attracting skunks into the neighborhood—it was bad enough when he was attracting pigeons, but skunks were worse. George again got mad about people trying to tell him how to run his backyard.

One weekend afternoon, Bob Simpson from across the street came over and asked George if it was true about the skunks. George said, "Sure, they come up on the deck, and we give them a few bites."

Bob, whom George liked, thought this was really amazing. He asked George if he could come over some night to watch the skunks.

"Sure," George said, "why don't you bring Helen over tonight, and we'll have a few martinis and watch the skunks? If they don't show up, you can help me watch the Mets."

About the beginning of the second martini, a skunk made his way through the backyard and up onto the deck, followed by another skunk. Helen Simpson was petrified. Bob was a little nervous and knocked over a metal ashtray which hit the deck, right next to the skunks, with a loud clang. The skunks looked up momentarily, but, unbothered, went back to eating.

Things got very uptight again when George went into the kitchen to mix some drinks and forgot to close the door. One of the skunks climbed the sill and disappeared into the kitchen.

George told everybody not to worry. There wasn't any food in the kitchen, so the skunk would be right back out. After a few minutes, though, they could see the skunk sniffing around in the living room.

George was sure he knew how to work this out. He went around the house and opened the front door, figuring the skunk would find his way out. Instead, the skunk took off down some stairs and was investigating the studio where George and Jane worked on their paintings. There were a lot of Jane's paintings down there, framed and ready for a show coming up soon.

Thinking that all the skunk had to do was squirt one of Jane's paintings and he'd never hear the end of it, George crept down the stairs after the skunk, trying not to make any sudden noises. He decided he'd better have some kind of sound going when he finally came up behind the skunk, so he started talking:

"Look, man, you're in the wrong place. C'mon now, man, you've got to get out of here. You're going to get me in trouble with my wife. Man, if you get me in trouble with my wife, I'll have to knock off the Fritos and the other stuff, and you won't get to hang around our backyard anymore."

With George close behind and keeping up a pleading lecture, the skunk made his way quietly out the front door.

"Nothing to it," George announced. "It just goes to show you these little animals aren't hard to get along with if you just act natural."

The Simpson's figured maybe they'd had too much to drink or something. They thanked the Reicharts and left. George thought it was rather early for them to leave, the way they liked martinis and all.

Even though Bob Simpson told the skunk story around the neighborhood exactly the way it happened, wouldn't you know that the way it finally came out was that the Reicharts had a real, live, unfixed skunk living right inside the house?

For once, George was unbothered by what the neighbors said; he really had it going now, from earliest morning until midnight or later. At dawn, there were the woodpeckers whose staccato drilling was somehow a more natural wake-up call than the civilized clanging of the alarm clock, which he had stopped using. At breakfast and again through cocktail time and supper on weekdays and all through the weekends, there were all the other little creatures, the birds, especially—even the untidy, ghetto-flown pigeons. Life was filled with pleasant sights and sounds.

For awhile, anyway.

52

CHAPTER EIGHT

Although George could not have known it immediately, the pleasantness began to sour when Ed James was transferred to South America. George liked Ed about as well as he could like anybody who trapped squirrels, but he was relieved to know that Ed was leaving.

There was a neighborhood farewell party for Ed James, of course, and later on a welcoming party for the new neighbor, a dentist named Jim Atkinson, who specialized in root-canal work. George was never comfortable around Jim Atkinson. Everytime they met, George got to thinking about that root-canal business, and his teeth began to hurt. Even so, he figured Jim had to be an improvement over Ed James. George was disastrously wrong.

Jim quickly got onto everything that had been going on about the woodpeckers, the squirrels, the pigeons, and the other birds and now the skunks, and he got a cat.

It was a big female with orange and white stripes

and spotted all over with black that George called Calico Cat. Apparently nobody fed Calico Cat very much—deliberately, George was sure—because she spent most of the day in the Reichart backyard stalking everything that moved.

George kept putting out all the food, but it was just like putting out a smorgasbord because one day the cat would catch a blue jay and the next a sparrow. Soon, there were feathers all over the yard.

George was bewildered. If he quit putting out food for the birds, perhaps they'd go away. But if they went away, especially now that winter was near, they might starve to death.

Then George's next-door neighbor on the other side, Kendall King, got a cat, too. The Kiersted family, across the street, turned up a real tough, black tomcat that got into so many fights he finally ended up with one eye.

Two doors down the street, another neighbor got a cat. Now, there were six or seven cats living right around the Reichart house and spending most of their time in the Reicharts' backyard.

George was mad, but he doesn't get mad the way most people do; he doesn't curse or yell or pound his fist or stamp his feet. His voice takes on a hurt, bewildered tone as though he can't believe that all this is happening to him, and he doesn't understand why.

"It's my backyard," he told Jane, his voice puzzled and shaky. "Why should the neighbors try to tell me what I can or can't do with it? I'll bet they all got the cats just to get at me."

"Of course they did," Jane agreed. "The way they look at it, if you have a right to bring woodpeckers and pigeons and a lot of animals they don't like into the neighborhood, they have a right to bring in cats to chase them out."

George didn't answer. He didn't know what to say or think.

A few days later at work, a premium salesman called on George. He had a bunch of bird and small animal calls and an idea. For one dollar along with the purchase of a package of White Owls (an owl is a bird, too), you could get an Audubon call that would entice all sorts of beautiful feathered creatures, or a duck call, or a goose call, or a crow call, together with a little booklet telling you how to be a woodland Pied Piper.

The crow call gave George a sneaky idea for how he could get back at the neighbors. He was thinking about some crows he saw hanging around the garbage cans behind the supermarket and a restaurant down the hill from his backyard, where the swampy stream and the ducks had been when the Reicharts moved in. He saw the crows down there on Sundays while walking Ichabod. Sunday, when everything was closed and there were no people around, seemed to be the only time they had a chance at the garbage cans.

The next Sunday morning, George stood out in the backyard all bundled up against the cold, field-testing the premium salesman's crow call. He blew the thing like it said in the little booklet. It made a kind of rubbery, cawing sound. George would blow a couple of caws and stand around shivering and waiting for something to happen. Finally—right after he blew three short, consecutive caws—first one crow, then another landed on a tree limb at the back of the yard. They sat there for awhile, wary and watchful. Then one of them swooped down, grabbed one of the chunks of meat George had scattered around and flew off. Then the other did the same thing.

In a little while, there were some more crows. And some more. All cawing at each other and at George, who was cawing back at them, so that the little back-yard in the quiet Scarsdale neighborhood sounded like an abandoned cornfield at harvest.

About as fast as a crow can fly, word got around the neighborhood that George Reichart was up to something. If there was any doubt about what George was up to, it was soon dispelled by the Kimballs' little boy, Kirk, and the Thomases' little girl, Michele. They were about twelve years old and collaborated on a little neighborhood newspaper. If somebody's lawn had a hole in it because somebody else coming home late from a party drove up on the sidewalk, that would be in the paper. Or if somebody's teen-age son took somebody else's teen-age daughter to the high-school prom, but didn't ask her for a date the next week, that would be there, too. The little paper was full of all kinds of news, and all up and down Westminster Road, it got more readership than the advertising column in the *New York Times*.

"Attention Crow Haters," said the little paper's headline right after George's first adventure as a crow caller. "Mr. Reichart is feeding crows in his backyard. He's giving them all kinds of meat and stuff. We thought you should know this."

Jane thought it was very funny and airmailed the paper to Jan, by now graduated from college, newly married, and living in Arizona.

George thought it was funny, too. But in a way it was sad because the kids' newspaper reflected a kind of neighborhood establishment view. The way he looked at it, the paper should have said, "Look what Mr. Reichart is doing, and isn't it wonderful? This is something the whole neighborhood should be doing." After all, nobody in the neighborhood had a cornfield or anything else to protect.

All that winter George got out his crow call every Sunday morning and cawed up all the crows within range. As it turned out, it was one of the coldest winters in years. There was snow on the ground most of the time and ice and freezing winds. The people in the neighborhood were kept busy shoveling their driveways, chipping ice off the sidewalks, and trying to get their cars started. It was so cold and miserable

57

that the cats stayed home most of the time. But the pigeons and sparrows and crows and some other birds that didn't have the sense to fly south—and some squirrels and rabbits and chipmunks—seemed hungrier than ever. George saw to it that they had plenty to eat.

CHAPTER NINE

At the first signs of spring, all the cats in the neighborhood came out of their houses and headed for George's backyard.

Calico Cat, from next door, came earliest and stayed longest. She spent all day lurking behind the bushes and trees. Every once in awhile, she pounced —and there would only be a bunch of feathers where she landed.

There was a tomcat from down the street, all white except for a comical-looking black swatch under his nose, that George called Hitler. He specialized in chipmunks. There was Vishinsky, a mangy-looking, dirty white cat with a crooked tail. Vishinsky favored blue jays. Inky, the big black tomcat from across the street, went after everything—including Ichabod.

And there were some females with little plastic collars around their necks which belonged to Fred Kimball. There were also some kittens, apparently undergoing their basic training in the Reicharts' backyard.

One of them, all gray except for a splash of orange fur across her forehead, belonged to Calico Cat.

The blue jays, the ones that managed to stay out of the cats' clutches, disappeared or stayed up in the trees. So did the robins. The sparrows and pigeons were around, but they weren't exactly loitering over their meals. For awhile the crows kept coming, but now they just sat up in the tree limbs looking things over.

Most of the chipmunks wound up inside the cats. The squirrels stayed up in the trees, except for those not old enough to be wary.

Even the woodpeckers were threatened. The cats tried to climb the trees onto the low hanging branches where their food hung in mesh bags. One morning Calico Cat tried to shinny up a drainpipe to get at a woodpecker up near the roof.

George's noisy, little-creature wonderland was almost still. There were occasional bright sounds, but too often they ended up in shrill, tiny screams of terror, then silence.

George was helpless. He tried running out into the yard to scare off the cats, but all the other animals ran away or flew off. The cats never went very far. They just darted into the bushes or ducked behind the trees to wait things out. Except Calico Cat. She just moved onto the terrace and sat on her haunches staring at George as though *he* was the intruder.

George tried another tactic. He collected some rocks and lined them up on the window ledge outside the kitchen. When he spied a cat entering the yard, George would yank open the back door, grab a rock and hurl it at the cat.

That upset Jane. "What are you doing that for?" she asked George. "The neighbors are mad enough as it is; if you hurt one of their cats, they're going to be even madder. Besides, you can't stay home from work every day just to throw rocks at the cats."

George wasn't really mad at the cats. He was mad at the neighbors. He was sure they bought the cats purposely to chase, or kill off, the birds and animals in his backyard. The way George looked at it, they were dwindling in number anyway; the ones that were left ought to be protected or at least left alone. It was bad enough that people came, tore down the woods and built houses and stores and streets and sidewalks, causing most of the woodland creatures to run and fly for their lives. That, he supposed was the way civilization worked. But when they turned loose the cats to feed off the ones that were left, that was murderous.

The remarkable thing about the war between George and his neighbors was that it never really carried beyond the boundaries of his backyard; otherwise the people in the neighborhood, including George and Jane, played bridge together, went to the same parties and visited back and forth.

There was even a big party for George to celebrate his company's announcement that he had been elected a vice-president. That was when George, his confidence buffered by a couple of martinis, had a talk with Fred Kimball about his three cats with the plastic collars.

"They're flea collars," Fred explained. "You put those collars on the cats, and somehow the fleas don't bother them anymore."

"I was thinking about those collars," George said. "Why don't you tie little bells on the collars? Then when your cats come running over into my yard, the bells will scare all the birds and animals away, and your cats won't be a menace anymore."

"I guess you don't know anything about cats," Fred told George. "You put a bell on a cat and it makes him neurotic or something. He gets all shook up."

George dropped the subject, but later in the evening Fred brought it up again.

"I've been thinking about those bells and I have an idea. You know those pigeons of yours? They stop by my home on the way to your house, and they've got the roof all messed up."

George said he couldn't very well help that. He supposed even a pigeon has to stop somewhere to take a breather.

"Sure," Fred agreed. "Anyhow, here's my idea. I'll put bells on all the cats—like you said, George—if you'll put diapers on those goddamned pigeons."

That was George's last attempt at a cocktail party solution; the way he looked at it, nobody ever made much sense at a cocktail party anyhow. "You know something," he told Jane later, "I should have told

Fred to put his cats out on the roof all day. That way, the pigeons wouldn't land there, and his cats wouldn't come over here."

Instead, the Kimball cats were coming over to the Reichart backyard earlier than before—and staying longer—as if in retaliation for George wanting to put bells on their collars. They huddled in the air space underneath the big redwood deck at the back of the house; sometimes hiding there for hours until the terrace at the other end of the yard was crowded with hungry and unsuspecting little animals. Then one of them or two or even all three, crept out into the open, crawled the length of the yard, alternately moving and waiting motionless, and leaped into the midst of the feeding animals.

George thought of rigging up some kind of a wire with a loud buzzer on one end, so he could press a button inside the house, and the buzzer, hidden under the deck where the cats huddled, would sound off and scare them away. Not being an electrician, he never worked it out. One morning, enraged, he burst through the open kitchen door and launched into a running broad jump. He landed with a jarring thump on the boards above where the cats were hiding, screaming "Yeeooowww!" The birds flew off, the chipmunks dived into their little tunnels, the squirrels disappeared up in the trees. The cats streaked around a corner of the house, but in less than an hour they were back at their posts. Jane wondered how the people at George's company would feel about their newest vice-president leaping around on his back porch screaming.

Still refusing to concede defeat, George reasoned that if he tricked the Kimball cats into associating their hideout with something unpleasant, they might not come back. He stationed Jane in front of a narrow horizontal window in the basement where she could see underneath the deck. He filled a bucket with water, opened the kitchen door and hurled the water, bucket and all, across the desk, so it would flood down through the cracks between the boards onto the cats, and that would be the end of that hideout. "The water went one way," Jane reported from her lookout in the basement. "The cats went the other way—dry."

It had become a deadly contest between the Kimball cats, and Calico Cat, Vishinsky, and all the other cats in the neighborhood—the females particularly —to see who could get to the Reichart backyard earliest and stay the longest and leave the most feathers lying around.

It was a terrible spring for George. He could only imagine that summer would be worse.

CHAPTER TEN

It grew worse all too soon, on a Friday morning when George went down into the garage to back the car out so Jane could drive him to the station.

He stared at the car, unbelieving. There were muddy footprints all over it, all over the hood and the roof and the fenders. They were put there by a cat or two cats or three cats.

The car had been locked inside the garage all night; there were no windows or doors open anywhere in the house. George was bewildered.

On and off all day he wondered about the footprints. He thought about all the ghost stories he had ever heard, which he didn't believe anyhow, but he wondered now if they could be true and if there was such a thing as a cat ghost. He decided probably he had fallen asleep on the train on the way into the city and only dreamed about the footprints. He called Jane to ask if she had figured out yet how the footprints got all over the car, hoping she would ask, "WHAT footprints?" No, Jane said, she hadn't figured it out, but she had sponged them off the car so George might as well go back to work and forget about it.

By evening, Jane had worked out an answer. There was no mystery about it at all. Probably when George put the car in the garage the night before, he forgot for awhile to throw the remote switch in the kitchen, which closed the garage door. It made sense because George often forgot the switch until late at night, and a couple of times he had forgotten it altogether.

The next morning, not fully awake, George went downstairs early to put out some meat for the crows and make some coffee. There was Calico Cat, sitting on the carpet in the middle of the living room, hunched over a big piece of meat. George came awake fast. He let out a yell, and Calico Cat streaked through the kitchen and down into the cellar. George started after the cat but thought of a better idea. He closed the cellar door—and smiled. Now he was going to call Jim Atkinson and tell him to come over and get his cat and keep the thing at home from now on.

Jane didn't think that was a good idea. Suppose Jim Atkinson came downstairs some morning and found one of George's skunks in his living room or a crow or a bunch of pigeons. Jane was looking out into the backyard now, and George saw the look of surprise on her face. "Besides," she asked George, "can you really prove you saw the cat in the living room this morning?" George looked, too—at Calico

70

Cat, sitting out on the deck, staring through the window at George.

George searched the house. He checked all the windows and doors; he backed the car out and moved around inside the garage, looking for an opening big enough for a cat to sneak through; searching, in a way, for proof of his sanity. He found the place, finally, an open vent high up the wall near the back of the cellar. He traced the vent outside the house. There were marks in the soft earth, cat scratches, he was sure.

That vindicated George, of course, but it also served to make him rant all the more about cats that not only ran around killing birds and other animals but got into his garage at night and muddied his car and now even sneaked into the kitchen to steal the crows' food.

Jane didn't think the cats were to blame, or even their owners; it was their own fault for leaving the vent open. Nor was it the cats' fault that they stalked the birds and the squirrels and so forth. Cats are predators. It is natural for them to stalk and catch birds and little animals; the same way it is natural for the birds and little animals to chase and catch bugs and worms. "All it is," Jane explained to George, "is the balance of nature."

George did some thinking about the balance of nature and how he could put it to work for him. What he needed was some kind of animal that would chase cats, but wouldn't scare away the other animals. Some kind of bird maybe, but whoever heard of a bird that chased cats?

Finally, George remembered a very unusual bird, from another time, in a very unusual place. The place was a tiny mountain village in China in the year 1935, where George had a job teaching English to the children of Lau Ai Gee, a wealthy Chinese businessman. He had worked his way from California to China on a succession of freight ships to catch up with a tall blonde girl named Jane Carlson, a college friend.

In the summer, the family of Lau Ai Gee moved from their home on an island in the Min River, to the cool heights of the village of Kuliang in the Fukien mountains, where they had a compound of stone houses in the pine forests. There George tutored the Lau children and the children of his summer guests, as many as twelve or fourteen at a time. He also went out to the edge of the compound every morning to retrieve the mail, dropped on the road by a postman too scared to go near the houses.

What scared the mailman was a pet goose, almost as big as an ostrich, which belonged to a visiting family from Shanghai. They had brought along some goats, too, and some chickens, but the goose wasn't kept outside with the rest of the animals. She wandered around the front yard or sat on the porch near the kitchen door, more pet than poultry. If a strange animal entered the yard, the goose spread her enormous wings and, half-running, half-flying, hissing fiercely, took off after the animal. If a stranger arrived, the goose had to be locked up; she seemed to know who belonged in the compound and guarded it like a watchdog. A couple of times, she got the mailman in the seat of his khaki shorts.

All these years later in Scarsdale, George could not be sure what made him think of the goose from China, or why he had not thought of it before.

CHAPTER ELEVEN

George found the place, finally, in Connecticut, just above the New York State line. The sign out front said it was Sherwood Farm.

There was a farmhouse standing back from the road with a pond out front filled with geese and wild ducks. There were chickens massed in the backyard and turkeys and even some peacocks. George thought to himself, "Wow, this is the place! I've got to talk to this guy."

George told the farmer he was interested in buying a goose to keep as a pet, but first he had to know whether a goose would chase cats.

Probably, the farmer said, a goose that could lay eggs and have goslings might chase cats. Not a gander, though; the female seemed to be more protective than the male.

George walked around the pond with the farmer, examining the geese. He finally picked one that was smaller and younger than some of the others, but one that looked more alert and seemed to move faster.

It was predominantly a light-grayish tan with darker streaks of brown and gray on its wings, and thick orange-colored legs and feet. He asked the farmer many questions about the care and feeding of a goose, bought a big bag of mash and drove home with the goose squatting quietly in a wooden crate in the back of the station wagon.

Jane was silent. She had been appalled at the idea of buying the goose. She worried that the goose would mess up the backyard. George said that was all right, what good was the backyard, anyhow, when it was always full of cats?

Suppose the goose had some goslings, who was going to look after them? "The goose, of course," George had answered. "Isn't that where the name Mother Goose came from?" The neighbors weren't going to like it; what if the goose wandered around in other people's yards? "Wonderful," George had said, "they come over and tell me to keep the goose out of their backyards; I tell them to keep their cats out of my yard."

Jane gave up finally. Her last words were that George had better look into the need for exercising the goose. She refused to walk it around the neighborhood on a leash, the way she used to walk Ichabod before he finally died of old age.

At first, George kept the goose penned up in a wire run he had built for Ichabod, so she would get the feeling of the place and not wander off when let loose.

Early one morning a few days later, he filled the goose's food tray with moistened mash, opened the gate of its pen, and slowly walked the tray onto the terrace, where the other animals' food had been spread out. The goose followed along eagerly, as if on an invisible leash. George hurried back into the kitchen, where he could witness whatever was going to happen next.

Some starlings flew down and pecked away at the food on the patio. Some doves arrived and then some blue jays and a couple of squirrels. The goose and the birds and the squirrels all were huddled out on the terrace, busily eating the food, unbothered by one another's presence.

In the kitchen, George was having some terrible second thoughts. Of one thing he was sure—a cat would show up soon. But what if the cat pounced and the goose paid no attention? Or suppose the cat pounced and the goose fled? Or—utter disaster—what if the goose and the cats made friends?

Here, in George's own words, is what did happen:

"Sure enough the first cat comes along. He sneaks up on the whole situation and sits for awhile. Then he sneaks up a little closer and sits again. Then he comes a little closer and he gets kind of twitchety. His front paws get to wriggling and he swishes his tail. He gets all ready to pounce, and the goose sees him and Oh, boy! This goose puts out its wings and it hisses and it takes off after that cat, and I never saw such a beautiful sight in my life. That cat streaked out of there—zip, like that—and I thought wow, have we got it made!"

One by one the other cats arrived, one by one they came flying out of the backyard, hair standing on end, tails rigid, ears folded back, as if speared by lightning. A little French poodle from up the street, one of those nervous, yappity kind that will challenge everything bustled into the yard and yapped at the goose. The goose took off after the poodle. He went running up Westminster Road, howling as though he had been chewed on by a lion. George wanted to hug the goose or pet her, but he doubted the goose would understand that. He stayed inside the house all day, cheering like a baseball fan for a home run every time a cat hurtled out of the yard.

Word about the goose sped through the neighborhood. Jim Atkinson from next door—the man who brought the first cat into the neighborhood —came over. "I see you've got a goose back here," he said to George.

George said, "Sure, it's a goose, all right."

"I was wondering," Atkinson said, "do you need a permit for a goose or a license or anything like that?" George backed out of that conversation fast, being sure that Jim Atkinson was going to call the police, and they'd come and take his goose away.

He called up the Scarsdale police station. "I need a little information," he told the policeman who answered the phone. "Dogs have to have a license, right? What about cats? Do they need a license or anything?" No, the policeman explained. Cats don't need a license. George asked how was it that a dog had to be licensed but not a cat. "Well," the policeman explained, "dogs are a large, dependable animal. People have to feed them. If they're not fed, they may be dangerous. Cats take care of themselves, even if they're not fed, they get around and catch birds and things."

"What about a goose?" George asked. "Supposing I have a goose in my backyard. Does it need a license?"

No, the policeman told George, a goose doesn't need a license. As a matter of fact, he once kept a duck in his backyard. The duck was a lot of fun.

What about the neighbors, George asked, did they get upset about the duck? Sure, the policeman said, the duck used to quack, and the neighbors would get sore, but he couldn't stop the duck from quacking, could he? and besides the neighbors couldn't do anything about it anyhow.

George was relieved. The cops couldn't come and take away his goose after all.

All summer the goose patrolled the Reichart backyard. The little animals that were still in the neighborhood, those who had survived the cats, and the ones which had not fled before the steam shovels and earthmovers and the hammering and sawing of civilization, were returning in numbers. The blue jays and sparrows were arriving in flocks. The crows came down from their perches in the trees. The pigeons were back, including the one with the missing foot that flopped onto its side when it landed and gimped around the yard after the food. George and Jane called him Pegleg. It seemed to them that while the rest of the animals moved freely around the yard, Pegleg never wandered too far from the goose. The squirrels came down out of the trees and gobbled up the sunflower seeds, as unbothered as they had been in the years before the cats.

The cats didn't give up completely. At least several times a day, there was a commotion in the backyard —the fierce sound of hissing and the angry rustle of wings. The birds flew off; the squirrels ran up into the trees. But they didn't fly or run very far now. In a little while, they were back in the yard, gathered around the goose, feeding or walking around or just sitting, secure and content.

CHAPTER TWELVE

Had it not been for George's first business trip to Europe, with the option of adding on to it a couple of weeks vacation with Jane, this little book might have ended here, with the goose standing guard over an effective, although sporadically noisy stalemate. It wasn't peace, exactly, but George was happy to settle for it.

The Reicharts lost themselves in travel brochures, maps, timetables, looking for a place to spend the last couple of weeks in December, after George completed his business. George was attracted to Switzerland because of its splendid scenery. Jane was looking for some place with a blander climate, Tunisia perhaps, as a respite against coming back to the snow and ice of Scarsdale in January.

The snow and ice—

The goose!

George and Jane were dismayed by this sudden complication to their own plans and embarrassed by their thoughtlessness. Obviously, you don't just bundle up a goose and drop it off at its grandparents' as you would a child. Probably you couldn't board a goose at the vet's either, certainly not this goose because of the way she felt about cats and some dogs, too. Jane thought about the Sherwood Farm, where they bought the goose. Maybe it could be boarded there.

George thought the goose deserved something better, a vacation far away from the everyday business of chasing cats, some place where it was warm all winter. He was thinking about Frank Warren, an old friend who had retired from George's company and was living in Florida, near Sarasota, in a beautiful house that faced an inlet, with a great stretch of lawn between the house and the water. On his last trip to Florida, George had visited Frank and his wife, Janet, so he knew what a perfect place it would be for the goose to spend the winter. There were wildfowl along the inlet and some pelicans, so the goose would not lack company.

Frank Warren didn't show any surprise when George called to explain the situation. He had known George too long for that, but he thought it was pretty funny. "Sure," he told George after talking it over with Janet. "You send the goose down by air, if that's the way you're going to do it, and we'll pick it up at the Tampa airport."

George wasn't sure about shipping the goose by air, though. He knew that people shipped dogs and

cats back and forth by air and that racehorses sometimes travel by air. A goose, though, might be a problem. He thought of calling up an airline to ask how
to fly a goose, but decided not to; whoever answered
the phone might think he was crazy and hang up.
Instead, he drove over to Westchester Airport, assum-
ing that someone there could tell him just as much
about flying a goose as anybody at La Guardia or
Kennedy, which were much farther away. He
checked the departure boards in the airport; the farthest south anybody went was Mohawk Airlines to
Washington, D.C. George waited around until there
was no one at the Mohawk counter except the clerk.
He eased up to the counter, with Jane close behind,
and in a very offhand tone, George said to the clerk,
"I want to fly a goose to Washington." The clerk
looked like he was sure something had gone wrong
with his hearing. "I mean," George explained, "I
want some information about sending a goose to
Washington by air."

The clerk, who could be as offhand as anybody else,
asked George if he had a kennel.

It was George's turn to look like something had
gone wrong with his hearing. "A kennel?" he asked,
puzzled. "This is a goose." It took quite a few questions back and forth to settle on the fact that George
would provide his own shipping container.

The clerk, searching around behind the counter for
some manual or other that would get him out of this,

wanted to know how much the goose weighed. He said he thought these things went by weight.

George did some doodling on a little pad he had brought along to record all the information. "Well," George said, "he—I mean she—has big fat legs. I guess the legs weigh five pounds each and the rest of her weighs another twenty pounds, maybe twenty-five. That's thirty, maybe thirty-five pounds. The crate weights ten pounds, maybe fifteen. That brings it up to fifty pounds, give or take a few pounds. Maybe ten pounds one way or the other."

The clerk called to another clerk for help, as airlines people so often do. Between them, they came up with a figure of eighteen dollars, minimum, to fly the goose to Washington.

George, who was only beginning to warm up to the investigation, asked, "Where does the goose fly?" He thought that sounded mixed up, so he rephrased it. "I mean, where do you put the goose?"

The second clerk said the goose would fly down in the baggage compartment, of course. He must have thought that sounded all mixed up, so he started over. "I mean," he explained, "we take the crate with the goose inside, and we put it in the baggage compartment."

George didn't like the sound of that. "Won't the goose freeze to death down there?" he wanted to know. The first clerk, back on safe ground, said of course not, the temperature was the same as in the cabin.

86

George, who appeared to be copying down everything that was said, now wanted to know if he needed a health certificate or a permit or anything like that to fly the goose or rather to ship it. The two clerks called upon a third man whose name was Charlie. The way Charlie took over, George thought he must be a supervisor. Charlie said it might be a health problem if you were flying some tropical birds into the country or importing a bunch of monkeys, but flying a goose from one place to another inside the country, that was no problem at all. "A goose," he explained, reading from an airline reference book, "a goose is a poultry."

Now that he had the entire Mohawk staff at his disposal, George was not going to miss any opportunities for expert advice. He said he had heard that people who shipped dogs by air sometimes gave them a shot, a tranquilizer or something. One of the clerks told George this was something he should take up with a veterinarian.

Jane said she didn't think the goose would need a tranquilizer. "After all," she explained, "a goose is used to flying."

The clerk looked all around the airport, which was almost deserted, at all the walls and even up toward the ceiling. "You know," he whispered to one of the other clerks, "I have a feeling there's a television camera around here somewhere."

There was something else George wanted to be sure of. Whenever he traveled by air, he had to have his name on a ticket. This ticket, or whatever it was that went along with the goose, did it have to have the goose's name on it? Jane was hoping that George wouldn't go into a long explanation of how they had run through a lot of people names like Penelope and Gertrude, and some action names like Scat and Swoosh, but because the goose wouldn't have answered to a name anyhow, they finally called her simply Mother Goose.

His tone of voice clearly indicating that if there were any more questions he wasn't going to be around to answer them, the first clerk told George to bring his goose, crated, to the airport and just fill out all the forms, and it wouldn't be any problem at all. Out loud, he said to one of the other clerks, "I'm positive there's a television camera around here. There has to be."

A few days later, George and Jane coaxed the goose into a big crate which George had built and hauled it over to La Guardia airport, to be put aboard an Eastern Airlines flight to Tampa. When the shipping clerk lifted the crate onto a baggage wagon, and another started to haul it toward the runway, the goose sat quietly, looking confused and reproachful.

Jane's eyes filled with tears. George felt the need for a drink.

That evening, Frank Warren called from Florida to say that the goose had arrived in fine shape and quickly made herself at home. She was out near the inlet now, grazing on the lawn. At the cocktail party going on at Frank's house there was a great deal of conversation about the goose that came to Florida for the winter to rest up from chasing cats all summer.

George and Jane felt better—but only a little better.

CHAPTER THIRTEEN

Early in December, the Reicharts went off on their trip to London, Paris, Copenhagen, and Antwerp. They spent Christmas and New Year's in Tunisia vacationing. Along the way, George sent some postcards to the Warrens and a few addressed to the goose. One, from the town of Nefta in Tunisia, told the goose how George had almost bought a baby camel for thirty-five dollars at an auction. He had been inquiring into shipping costs when Jane caught up to him, which was too bad because he thought the baby camel and the goose would have hit it off just fine.

They arrived in Scarsdale on a Sunday early in January, in the midst of an ice storm. For all the rest of that month and the next, the weather was terrible; if anything, there was more snow and ice and freezing winds than the year before. Every day, they checked the weather reports for the west coast of Florida. It was almost always warm there, so the goose was having a fine, restful winter. In a sense, George was somewhat grateful for the bad weather in Scarsdale; it kept the cats at home most of the time. They did come over once in awhile, though, so George kept a supply of rocks lined up on the windowsill.

In the early part of March, George realized the time was near to send for the goose. He could tell this not so much because the iciness had gone out of the winds 'and the snow was melting into the ground, as by the increasing number of cats in the backyard. They were showing up more often now and staying longer. Calico Cat, who was in and out of the place most of the winter, was there all day now. Her kitten, now almost full grown, was there too—acting more and more like her mother. Vishinsky was back. So was Inky.

Early one Sunday morning toward the last week in March, George found a tiny heap of velvety, deep-red feathers in the yard, the male remains of a pair of cardinals which had first appeared in the yard a few days before. It was time to send for the goose.

George knew that something had gone wrong by the way Janet Warren answered the phone. She sounded worried and frightened. The goose had disappeared, just yesterday. The neighborhood children were searching the area; Frank was going up and down both sides of the inlet in a boat, looking for the goose. There was no sign of her. It didn't appear that she had been hurt or killed by some other animal. All George could think to tell Janet was not to worry—surely the goose would turn up in the next day or two—and to call Scarsdale as soon as she had any information, good or bad.

Jane burst into tears, which puzzled George. He reminded Jane that she hadn't wanted the darned goose in the first place. "I know," she managed to say in between fits of crying, "but it's like the time the squirrels disappeared from the birdhouse."

The days that followed were miserable. George found it almost impossible to concentrate on his work; in meetings, his mind wandered far from the subject, lost in speculation. Jane started a number of paintings, but couldn't finish any one of them. They called back and forth several times a day to check on whether there was any news from Florida. There was none.

George had an idea of what happened to the goose. There were alligators all over Florida, he knew. If an alligator had come up out of the inlet onto the Warren's property, the goose's sense of protectiveness might have caused her to take off after the alligator. If that had happened, it was surely the end of the goose.

The war in the Reichart backyard was going full blast again, although it was so one-sided now, it was more of a massacre. Having become accustomed to protection, the blue jays and the sparrows and all the other birds and animals entered the backyard innocently—not knowing there was no one there to protect them. The cats were having a field day. One evening George counted nine of them, including two new and fiercely aggressive female kittens, dispersed in hiding places around the yard. The terrace out back and the grass around it was cluttered with little bunches of feathers. Pegleg, the pigeon, was gone. Jane saw him land in the yard and roll over onto his stump. Before he could recover, one of the Kimball cats was on top of him.

The Reicharts lost all hope of hearing any good news from Sarasota. They talked about buying another goose, but decided not to, just as a few years before they had decided against trying to find another dog to replace Ichabod. There just wasn't another dog like Ichabod, or a goose like this one.

Jane was sure there was only one solution, hard as it might be for George to accept. If George was really concerned about keeping the birds and other animals alive, he must stop feeding them. About all he accomplished now, everytime he put food out for them, was to set them up for the cats. If he stopped, in time they would disappear. They would find food elsewhere, perhaps some place further away, where there were still some woods, where there were fewer houses and people, and cats were nonexistent or scarce.

It was a logical way to end things, George realized, and inevitable, but harder to accept than Jane or anyone else could possibly know. For years now, more than ten, he had been putting out the sunflower seeds for the squirrels, spreading seed for the birds and filling their trays, and preparing the meat and bones and suet for the crows and woodpeckers—and putting out water for everybody. For all these same years, he had taken his place every morning at the kitchen table, watching and listening as the little creatures moved around the backyard or in the trees close to the ground or up on the trays, contentedly pecking or nibbling or chewing, not bothering anyone.

So matters stood one weekday morning when George came downstairs early to start the coffee. He heard a commotion in the backyard and glanced out the kitchen window. Here is what George saw, again in his own words:

"I absolutely couldn't believe it! There was a bunch of geese out back, six or seven of them. They were wild geese, except one of them wasn't a wild goose. It was our goose. I called Jane and told her to come downstairs fast, that she wouldn't believe what was going on. We went out in the backyard and sure enough the geese walked back into the woods, suspicious. Except one goose, the one that was our goose. She came running toward us with her neck stretched out in our direction, right up onto the deck like she was telling us she was glad to be home but she was hungry and where was the food?"

It was running through George's mind, that everybody who fights on one side or the other of a war believes that God is on his side. He never thought about God being on his side in his war with the neighbors, because he didn't go to church nearly as often as they did, but perhaps there was a divinity who looked after little creatures, who must have awakened some ancient instinct in the goose and nurtured it airborne, and helped it cross the endless miles—though no one will ever know how many stops there were for food and water and rest—who joined it here and there along the way with its wild kin and guided it, divinely, to its final landing in the tiny backyard in Scarsdale, to its guardian post on the beleaguered terrace.

George and Jane were standing out in the backyard, staring at the goose, unbelieving.

George felt a great, choking lump in his throat.

Jane cried.